Mathematics and Computing/Technology
An Inter-faculty Second Level Course
MT262 Putting Computer Systems to Work

Block III
Developing Visual Programs

Unit 3
Graphical Output

Prepared for the Course Team by Bob Margolis

This text forms part of the Open University second-level course MT262 *Putting Computer Systems to Work*, which among other things teaches the use of Borland C++Builder 5 Standard to tackle small programming projects. (Borland C++Builder 5 Standard is copyright © 2000 Borland International (UK) Limited.)

The course software comprises the Borland C++Builder 5 Standard CD-ROM and the MT262 Templates and Libraries CD-ROM, both of which are supplied as part of the course.

This publication forms part of an Open University course. Details of this and other Open University courses can be obtained from the Course Information and Advice Centre, PO Box 724, The Open University, Milton Keynes, MK7 6ZS, United Kingdom: tel. +44 (0)1908 653231, e-mail general-enquiries@open.ac.uk

Alternatively, you may visit the Open University website at http://www.open.ac.uk where you can learn more about the wide range of courses and packs offered at all levels by The Open University.

To purchase a selection of Open University course materials, visit the webshop at www.ouw.co.uk, or contact Open University Worldwide, Michael Young Building, Walton Hall, Milton Keynes, MK7 6AA, United Kingdom, for a brochure: tel. +44 (0)1908 858785, fax +44 (0)1908 858787, e-mail ouwenq@open.ac.uk

The Open University, Walton Hall, Milton Keynes, MK7 6AA.

First published 1999. Second edition 2002.

Copyright © 2002 The Open University

All rights reserved; no part of this publication may be reproduced, stored in a retrieval system, transmitted or utilised in any form or by any means, electronic, mechanical, photocopying, recording or otherwise, without written permission from the publisher or a licence from the Copyright Licensing Agency Ltd. Details of such licences (for reprographic reproduction) may be obtained from the Copyright Licensing Agency Ltd, 90 Tottenham Court Road, London W1T 4LP.

Open University course materials may also be made available in electronic formats for use by students of the University. All rights, including copyright and related rights and database rights, in electronic course materials and their contents are owned by or licensed to The Open University, or otherwise used by The Open University as permitted by applicable law.

In using electronic course materials and their contents you agree that your use will be solely for the purposes of following an Open University course of study or otherwise as licensed by The Open University or its assigns.

Except as permitted above you undertake not to copy, store in any medium (including electronic storage or use in a website), distribute, transmit or re-transmit, broadcast, modify or show in public such electronic materials in whole or in part without the prior written consent of The Open University or in accordance with the Copyright, Designs and Patents Act 1988.

Edited, designed and typeset by The Open University, using the Open University TeX System.

Printed in the United Kingdom by Martins the Printers, Berwick-upon-Tweed

ISBN 0 7492 4439 9

2.2

Contents

Introduction		4
1 Monitoring		6
2 Data logging		12
	2.1 A first solution	13
	2.2 File dialogs	15
3 A log file viewer		23
4 Data display		26
Objectives		34
Solutions to the Exercises		35
Solutions to the Computer Activities		43
Index		50

Study guide

A recommended study pattern, based on an average overall study time, is as follows.

Material	Study time
Introduction, Section 1 (computer)	$2\frac{1}{2}$ hours
Section 2 (computer)	5 hours
Section 3 (computer)	1 hour
Section 4 (computer)	2 hours

Note that all sections of this unit contain computer activities. If you have some study time when your computer is inaccessible, it should be possible to do the necessary design work for a particular section then, and do the practical work later.

This unit makes a number of course team versions of Builder projects available. These projects are complete, so that you may compile and run them in order to compare and check your coding of the designs against those of the course team.

All the C++ *coding* in the course team project files will be the same as yours is intended to be (apart from one or two intentional exceptions). What will be different are the `#include` lines that Builder inserts automatically, as well as some of the manually inserted lines. The reason is that course team file names are different from yours, being prefixed by CT. The course team felt that the advantage to you of being able to *run* the course team projects outweighed the disadvantage of having to cope with these slight differences.

Introduction

The main new ideas introduced in this unit are ones connected with the presentation of information in graphical, rather than text (string), form. In order to deal with graphical input and output, all the design and coding techniques introduced so far will be required, so you will gain further practice in using these techniques. For some of the problems encountered, it will be necessary to adapt existing classes by defining derived classes and using inheritance.

In the work that you have done to date, the graphical side has been purely the use of visual components such as buttons and menus. The actual information input as data or output as results has all been in the form of text, using edit boxes and memos. When working in some computing environments, only text is available for input and output. In many embedded computer systems, the options are even more limited: button presses for inputs and lights on or off for output (at least to the user). When PCs (and similar systems) are used for tasks such as monitoring industrial processes, it is often a good idea to present information

There will also be inputs from and outputs to the appliance that the embedded system controls.

graphically rather than as text. For example, presenting a temperature reading graphically usually makes it easier for the user to spot trends more quickly than if the readings are displayed as text.

Since the course team cannot assume that you have any actual measuring instruments attached to your computer, an additional Builder component has been provided which represents a 'dummy' measuring instrument. This component simulates a real temperature-measuring device to enable you to construct and test a visual interface. Providing you with this simulated instrument means that you can tackle problems involving the storage and graphical representation of data. In order to use the component, you will have to install it on the Builder Component Palette. This is, in itself, a useful skill to have, but the course will not be discussing how to *write* components to be installed in this way.

Part of the Builder Help system does cover writing components, albeit rather sketchily.

There are two main threads in this unit: developing ideas about measurements and their representation, and exploring the facilities that are available to implement these ideas. As with earlier work in this block, the ideas are applicable to any system where there are facilities for graphical output, but the implementation facilities are specific to the toolkit provided by Builder. However, similar facilities are offered for other graphical environments, including *X-Windows* (for *Unix*).

Section 1 tackles a problem of monitoring measurements from a single instrument. The design for a solution is approached in such a way that is as adaptable as possible. You have probably met many ways of representing information graphically: bar charts, line graphs and pie charts are all commonly used in print for such purposes. With computer monitoring, there is the added advantage of the display being able to follow the changes in the measurements displayed. Given the choices available, it is sensible to try to design solutions that will allow the user to change the particular form of display required without requiring a wholesale redesign of the solution. The design solution is then coded.

In order to make the dummy instrument component available, this section also deals with adding a component to the Builder Component Palette.

Section 2 looks at a very common requirement of computer monitoring systems: the ability to keep a permanent record of the measurements received. This is usually referred to as **data logging**. The solution discussed in Section 1 will have suitable file facilities added to it, in order to incorporate data logging. As well as the design ideas involved, this section will involve the use of Builder's components which represent standard dialog boxes for file opening.

Section 3 extends the solution developed in Sections 1 and 2. It also introduces some new ideas about windows that are displayed for particular purposes, rather than being available throughout the time that a program is running.

Finally, Section 4 introduces some further ideas about displaying data graphically.

1 Monitoring

In many situations, it is useful to have a computer system to monitor the readings that instruments are providing. In some industrial processes, adjustments have to be made to controls many times per second, based on information from instruments. This rate of response is simply too rapid to be carried out by human operators. In other cases, patient monitoring in hospitals being one, the problem may be operator boredom. It is not easy to maintain concentration over long periods, especially when little happens most of the time, but a rapid reaction to emergencies is required.

This section begins with a simplified task: displaying information from an instrument on the computer screen in an appropriate graphical form. The problem is then extended to cover automatically alerting the operator if a measurement strays outside a predetermined range.

There are two approaches to using instruments with computer systems: polling and interrupt-driven. In the *Windows* environment, an interrupt-driven approach (in which the instrument informs the system that a measurement is ready) is more likely to be used than a polling system (in which the program repeatedly asks the measuring instrument if a new measurement is available yet).

These two terms were introduced in *Unit 1*, Block I.

Problem Specification   Temperature Monitoring

A local electricity supply company has temperature-measuring instruments (thermometers) attached to equipment in the 'substations' that supply housing estates.

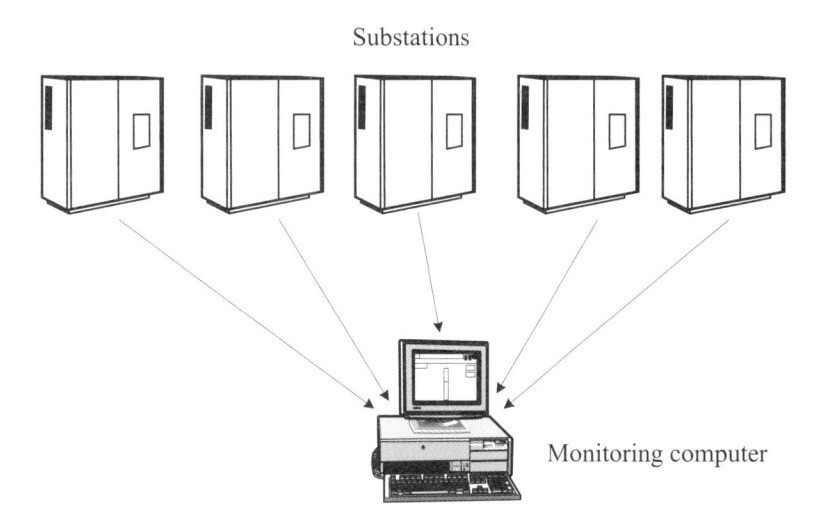

Substations

Monitoring computer

A monitoring system is required to display the information that is received, log all the data that is collected and alert operators if any temperature value lies outside safe limits. The temperature values produced by the thermometers will always lie in the range 20°C–160°C, but any measurement under 60°C or over 120°C indicates that there is a problem with the associated substation.

Initially, a prototype system is to be designed and coded which simply displays information from *one* thermometer. No warning system is to be implemented. The design and code should be capable of being extended: to more thermometers, to give warnings and to save data to files. The design and code should also allow the form of display to be changed easily in the light of users' reactions to the prototype system.

The thermometer supplier provides a dummy instrument in the form of a Builder component of type *TThermometer*. The properties, with their data types, and single event for this class are as follows. (There are no methods.)

Properties
- *Value*, **double**: the value of the last reading made by the instrument. (The value of this property may only be read at run-time, so it does not appear in the Object Inspector.)
- *Max*, **double**: the maximum measurement value, default value 100.
- *Min*, **double**: the minimum measurement value, default value 0.
- *Enabled*, **bool**: whether the instrument is making measurements, default value **false**.
- *Interval*, **int**: the time (in thousandths of a second) between measurements, default value 1000.

Events
- *OnTimer*, triggered when a fresh measurement is available, provided that *Enabled* is **true**. Occurs at the time intervals defined by *Interval*. When this event occurs, read *Value* to obtain the new measurement.

The *Max* and *Min* properties allow the programmer to set the range of temperatures that the instrument will measure. The *Interval* property is used to set how often measurements are taken. *Enabled* allows measurements to be started and stopped. □

This problem specification is fairly typical of a **prototype system**, that is, a system designed to test ideas that are intended to form part of a larger system. The initial requirement is for a very simple system. The only potential difficulty is in ensuring that the design is easy to extend — adding warnings or more thermometers, for example, should not require any redesign or recoding of work already done. You may have noted that the problem fits the 'visual interface plus engine' approach that has been used several times before. The thermometer component provides the engine. The problem is to provide a visual interface and to arrange proper communication between interface and engine. The solution to this problem will be tackled in the usual order: visual design, functional design, visual coding and other coding.

The initial visual design could be very simple: just a window with a display area. The program could run until closed by the user, and there seems to be no need for any of the usual *Windows* components such as menus, edit boxes and buttons. However, if this first solution is to be a useful prototype, it ought to have a menu (to be extended later), if only to provide a menu item for closing the program. It is also likely that a final system will use buttons for starting and stopping measurements, so this facility can usefully be incorporated now. In accordance with the ground rules laid down in the Appendix to *Unit 2*, the buttons should duplicate actions available through the menu (although the buttons will normally be the way the actions are invoked).

The various forms of display available have not been discussed. As you do the first exercise, you should consider what *you* would find the most useful form of display for temperature.

Exercise 1.1

Sketch a visual interface design for the prototype temperature monitoring system. Your design should be based on the discussion above and include the following components.

- a main menu
- a display
- buttons

A label might also be useful for your choice of temperature display.

[*Solution on page 35*]

The development of the design for temperature monitoring will be based on the course team's solution to Exercise 1.1.

With an initial visual design available, the next step is the functional design: what should happen when each menu item and button is chosen. There are also design decisions to be taken about initialisation. As part of designing initialisation, you should consider what should be initialised when the form is being designed (by setting properties) and what should be initialised by code.

Exercise 1.2

As with previous problems, initialisation has to deal with both visual and non-visual matters. Visually, you need to ensure that the program starts up in a sensible state. As far as non-visual items are concerned, the specification of the interface to the *TThermometer* component suggests that various properties ought to be initialised. Design this initialisation. Your design should be for a general measuring instrument component, not tied to the particular description of *TThermometer*.

Exercise 1.3

Design the action to be taken when the `Measurement|Start` menu item is chosen (or the `Start` button is pressed).

Exercise 1.4

Design the action to be taken when the `Measurement|Stop` menu item is chosen (or the `Stop` button is pressed).

Exercise 1.5

Design the action to be taken when a new measurement becomes available. This design will form the event handler for the thermometer's *OnTimer* event.

Exercise 1.6

Design the action to be taken when the `Exit` menu item is chosen.

[*Solutions on page 36*]

In fact, a little more needs to be said about what is to happen when the program closes. With a simulated measuring instrument, it is safe to do nothing when the program closes. With a real instrument, this is not true. A real instrument creates events (like the *OnTimer* event) by sending an electrical signal to the computer. If the code to deal with such events is not in place, then the operating system may, or may not, be able to cope. The safe course of action is to ensure that the instrument is disabled before the program closes.

Simply disabling the instrument in the event handler for the **Exit** menu item is not good enough, because *Windows* offers the user lots of ways to close a program. The programmer must ensure that each of these methods disables the instrument. When using Builder, the *OnDestroy* event is the counterpart for closing the program of the *OnCreate* event when the program starts. Thus, the instrument should be disabled in the *OnDestroy* event of the program's main form.

With the exception of the display component and thermometer, the designs just completed require only visual components that you have already used. Initially, the display will use a *TCGauge* component, located on the **Samples** tab of the Component Palette. (You will be asked to explore this and the *TThermometer* component shortly.) For now, you need to know that the *TCGauge* component has *MaxValue*, *MinValue* and *Progress* properties, which represent the maximum value to be displayed, the minimum value to be displayed and the current value, respectively.

Exercise 1.7

Use the following data table to refine the designs above (Exercises 1.2 to 1.6) so that they are ready for coding. Include a design for the *OnDestroy* event handler.

Type	Identifier	Description
TMenuItem	*FileMenu*	A menu
TMenuItem	*ExitItem*	Closes program
TMenuItem	*MeasurementMenu*	A menu
TMenuItem	*StartItem*	Starts measurements
TMenuItem	*StopItem*	Stops measurements
TButton	*StartButton*	Starts measurements
TButton	*StopButton*	Stops measurements
TCGauge	*TempGauge*	Displays current reading
TLabel	*GaugeLabel*	Labels gauge
TThermometer	*Thermometer*	Measuring instrument

[*Solution on page 37*]

In order to implement the designs that have been developed, you need to install the *TThermometer* component (provided by the course team) on the Component Palette. To do so, carry out the instructions overleaf.

- Start Builder (if necessary) and use `File|Close All` to close all open files.
- Choose `Component|Install Component...` from the main menu.
- Choose the upper `Browse` button in the dialog box that opens.
- Navigate to the `Block III` folder and choose `TThermom.cpp`. Click on `Open`. (Do *not* type in the name of the file, even if you know the full path to it. Builder will not do some additional housekeeping if you do so.)
- You will now be back at the first dialog box that appeared after choosing `Component|Install Component...`. Click on `OK`.
- A dialog box will open with a message about a package being built and then installed. Click on `Yes`.
- A fairly lengthy compiling activity will ensue. When complete, a dialog box will open with a message about a package having been installed. Click on `OK`.
- Use `File|Close All` to close the Code Editor window. In the dialog that appears next, concerning saving changes to project `dclusr50`, click on `Yes`.
- Check that the `Samples` tab of the Component Palette now has an icon representing a thermometer.

You now have the tools necessary for coding the designs in the solution to Exercise 1.7.

Computer Activity 1.1

Create a new application, and save it in the `Block III` folder using the names `Therm1U.cpp` for the form file, and `Therm1.bpr` for the project. Drop a main menu, two buttons, a label, a gauge and a thermometer (these last two from the `Samples` tab) onto the form.

TThermometer is one of a small collection of non-visual components which *can* be made fields of the form class by dragging and dropping.

Edit the menu so that it contains the menu as designed. Use the data table above to name the components and set captions appropriately. In particular, set the caption of the label to "Temperature", to explain what the gauge is registering (as in the visual design described earlier).

Name the form `ThermForm`, set its *Position* property to *poScreenCenter* and give it the caption "Thermal monitoring".

Alter the size of the gauge so that it looks like a vertical bar.

(a) What needs to be added to the event handler for the `File|Exit` menu item? Create the event handler skeleton, add the code, compile and check for correct operation.

(b) Investigate the *Kind* property of the gauge. Which value will enable you to use it for a vertical display as required by the design? Set the property appropriately. Set *MinValue* and *MaxValue* as in the initialisation design. Also set the *ShowText* property to **false** and set *Progress* to a value in the middle of the range to be displayed, say 90.

Compile and test this version.

(c) Check, using the Object Inspector, that the properties of the thermometer are as described earlier. Note the default values of the properties. (The *Value* property does not appear, as explained earlier.) Compile and test the program.

(d) Set any remaining initial property values (see the solution to Exercise 1.7), and test the revised version.

Computer Activity 1.2

(a) Create skeletons for the button *OnClick* event handlers (by double-clicking the buttons) and implement the designs already developed.

(b) Link the `Measurement|Start` and `Measurement|Stop` menu item event handlers to the button click event handlers already created. (See the solution if you cannot remember how to do this.)

(c) Create the *OnDestroy* event handler skeleton and add code to it to disable the thermometer component. Test the latest version.

[*Solutions on page 43*]

The remaining task is to deal with the *OnTimer* event so that the display is updated for each measurement.

Computer Activity 1.3

Create the event handler skeleton for the *OnTimer* event of the thermometer component. (Double-clicking on the component will do this because it has only the one event. Usually, double-clicking creates the handler for an *OnClick* event if it exists.) Add an assignment statement which assigns the *Value* property of the thermometer to the *Progress* property of the *TempGauge* display component. Compile and test the latest version. In particular, check the **Start** button, and observe the temperature display (of values generated randomly by *Thermometer*).

Computer Activity 1.4

This activity invites you to explore some additions to the monitoring program. You may well think of others that you would like to include; feel free to do so, but do not allow it to absorb *too* much time.

(a) Resizing the program window whilst the program is running may cause some of the components to be only partly visible. One solution to this problem is to fix the size of the window. You might try setting the form's *Width* property to 640, the *Height* property to 480 (guaranteed minimum screen size) and experimenting with the options for the *BorderStyle* property. You should find that at least one option prevents the user from resizing the window whilst the program is running.

(b) Labels could be added at the top and bottom of the display bar which give the maximum and minimum values.

(c) The colour of the vertical bar displayed in the gauge can be changed via the *ForeColor* and *BackColor* properties. You may wish to experiment with this.

(d) To add a warning feature, you could modify the *OnTimer* event handler to set the colour of the displayed bar. Green could be used for a measurement that was in the acceptable range, red for a value outside that range. To test this, you might wish to narrow the range of acceptable values. With the range in the original specification, unacceptable values are quite rare. You could also set *Interval* to give more than one measurement per second. Setting it to 100 (giving 10 measurements per second) might be helpful for testing.

(e) You may wish to investigate using other versions of the gauge component by changing the value of the *Kind* property. (You will probably want to move or remove any labels displaying maximum or minimum values if you do so.)

(f) Change the captions of menu items and buttons to include the & character for keyboard shortcuts.

(g) Instead of `Start` and `Stop` buttons, a single button could be used which changed its caption according to whether the next click started or stopped the measurements. The event handler would need an **if** statement, based on the current caption, to decide what action to take. To compensate for the additional code here, initialisation would be simpler.

[*Solutions on page 44*]

Part (b) of Computer Activity 1.4 raises an important issue about initialisation. So far, non-visual initialisation has been done in the *OnCreate* event handler and visual initialisation by setting properties in the Object Inspector. If labels for maximum and minimum measurements are added, there are three sets of initialisations connected with the range of measurement: of the thermometer, of the gauge and of the labels. A change in range involves searching through the project for all these. If any more features depending on the range were added, maintenance would become progressively more difficult. Thus, there is an argument which says that *any* initial values which are used in more than one place and which might be changed in maintenance should be set by code, not in the Object Inspector. It is *not* suggested that you go back and change your code, just that you should be aware of this issue.

This concludes a solution to the prototype monitoring problem. In fact, the section illustrates another point. The solution has been developed and tested with a simulated thermometer. This is a perfectly good way of designing and testing programs that will make use of specialised hardware attached to a computer system. The acceptability of the program to potential users can be assessed before purchasing real instruments (which may be a costly exercise). Likely extensions can be tested and checked to ensure that they would not make any extra demands on the actual measuring instrument(s).

Normally what is being tested is the visual user interface.

2 Data logging

This section considers the problem of extending the Temperature Monitoring problem to include a permanent record of measurements — that is, **data logging** is to be incorporated in the solution. This is a very common requirement in monitoring systems. The solution arrived at in Section 1 merely displayed each measurement as it became available, the actual measurements were lost. In the course of adding this new feature to the solution, some ideas about file operations will be introduced, as will the particular responsibilities that using files in *Windows* imposes on the programmer.

These responsibilities arise from the fact that *Windows* may be running several programs at the same time.

Disk files provide permanent storage, at least in the sense that the information that they contain does not disappear when the program closes, nor when the computer system is shut down.

To be specific, the following problem will be tackled in this section.

Problem Specification   Logging Temperatures

Extend the solution from Section 1 so that a disk file is produced containing a record of all measurements made. Each time the program is started up, new measurements should be *added* to the file.

For initial, testing purposes, the file on disk is to be called `TempLog.dat`.

Thus, the solution should be extended to allow the operator to do the following.
- Start and stop logging data to a file, independently of starting and stopping measurements.
- Specify the name of the disk file to be used for logging data.

□

The solution will be developed in two stages. The first subsection will tackle the problem to the stage where initial testing can be done with a fixed file name. In the second subsection the remaining features specified will be added.

2.1 A first solution

The solution to the original monitoring problem dealt with each measurement as it became available by displaying it. The first task is to identify where in the solution data logging should take place.

Exercise 2.1

Where in the solution already developed should the writing to the disk file take place?

[*Solution on page 37*]

An initial idea for the additional steps involved in data logging might be the following.
- open the data file with other initialisation when the program opens
- write each measurement to the file just before displaying it
- close the data file when the program closes

In a system using the *Windows* operating system, this is a rather 'antisocial' approach. There are a number of reasons for this assertion, but two are particularly important. Any open file uses some system resources from a pool that is shared by all programs that are running. It follows that a good general principle is to have files open for the minimum length of time required to carry out the task to hand. Second, other programs may wish to use the file that you have opened; there will be an example of this type later in this unit. Whilst it is possible to share access to files — essential for such things as databases with multiple users — life is easiest if files are kept opened for the minimum length of time. Thus, the file should be opened only when there is data to be written and closed immediately after writing. (So, opening the data file will *not* be part of the initialisation, as envisaged above.)

A socially acceptable design would be to add the following steps to the event handler for the *OnTimer* event handler in the original design.

1   open file
2   write new measurement to file
3   close file

In *Unit 4* of Block II, you met the `fstream` class library, which provides file facilities. When files are opened for writing (using objects of the *ofstream* class), any existing file of the name specified is destroyed. This will not do for the current task. What is needed is a way of preserving the existing file contents and adding the new measurement at the end. This is usually referred to as **appending** data to a file. The *ofstream* class provides an alternative form of the *open* method which opens an existing file non-destructively and prepares the file so that anything written to it is appended (that is, written at the end of existing data).

If the file named does not exist, it will be created.

The C++ statement required to open an *ofstream* object *LogFile* for appending, using the file name `TempLog.dat` is as follows.

`LogFile.open("TempLog.dat", ios::app);`

In this statement, the *open* method call has an extra parameter *ios::app*. The identifier *app* is for a constant integer that is defined in a module called *ios*, which is used internally by the `fstream` library. It is possible that other identifiers called *app* exist in one or more of the code libraries. It is for this reason that the 'full name' *ios::app* is used, so that the compiler understands that it is *app* from the *ios* module which is meant.

app is short for 'append'.

One further decision needs to be made: in what form should the data items be written to the file? Possibilities include writing the text representation (using the insertion operator `<<`) and writing the (binary) contents of memory using the *write* method. An important factor in such decisions should be the likely sizes of files. The text representation of a float or double takes about 7 characters and a new line requires 2 characters (in *Windows*). Thus, each measurement would require about 10 bytes. One measurement per second is 3600 per hour, so the log file would grow at the rate of about 36KB per hour. Even the modest storage capacity of a 1.44MB floppy disk would hold 40 hours' worth of data. Reducing the storage from 10 bytes per measurement to the four bytes of memory needed for a float is unlikely to be vital. The simplicity of the insertion operator makes it the course team's choice.

The *write* method approach was discussed in connection with the Warehouse problem in *Unit 4* of Block II.

The availability of resources affects such decisions. In a small computer system, a different view might have to be taken.

Exercise 2.2

Write down the C++ statements required to code the design for the statements to be added to the *OnTimer* event handler. Assume that the following declaration has been made somewhere in the project.

`ofstream LogFile;`

[*Solution on page 38*]

Computer Activity 2.1

Open the project `Therm1.bpr` and use `File|Save Project As...` to save it under the new name `Therm2.bpr`. Make sure that the form file `Therm1U.cpp` is the active tab in the Code Editor and then use `File|Save As...` to save it as `Therm2U.cpp`. (Builder will automatically rename the corresponding header file and bring the project makefile up to date.)

Add the code from the solution to Exercise 2.2 to the *Thermometer* component's *OnTimer* event handler. Add

`#include <fstream.h>`

after the other `#include` statements in `Therm2U.h`. Place the declaration of *LogFile* in the **private** section of the *TThermForm* class declaration (in `Therm2U.h`).

(a) Run the new version. Start measurements and allow them to continue for about 10 seconds. Stop measurements and close the program. Use `File|Open...` to open the file `TempLog.dat`. Count the number of data items in this file. Close the page in the Code Editor displaying the log file.

You will have to select `Any file (*.*)` in the `Files of type:` drop-down list, in order to see the file that you wish to open.

(b) Re-run the program, taking measurements for another 10 seconds or so. Re-open `TempLog.dat` in the Code Editor. Check that additional measurements have been appended to the file.

[*Solution on page 45*]

This concludes the initial stages of the data logging problem. Computer Activity 2.1 indicates that the logging is being done correctly.

You may have observed that the program provides no way to delete a file of measurements. In some systems this is an important feature, rather than a lack — permanent records of measurements may be essential for legal or security reasons.

You could find and delete the file using *Windows* utilities.

A serious restriction is that all measurements are added to the same file, there is no way of having separate files for, say, the measurements taken on different days. This issue will be discussed in the next subsection.

2.2 File dialogs

The task in this subsection is to add the features required by the problem specification that have not been implemented so far, beginning with the ability to start and stop logging.

The specification is not complete because it does not indicate whether the start and stop logging facilities should be provided by buttons or menus. Following the general guidelines, both will be provided, with the expectation that the buttons will be used most. This time, the approach will be to have a *single* button to start or stop logging and a menu item which duplicates the button's effect. The menu item is to be checked when logging is taking place.

Exercise 2.3

(a) Suggest a name for the new menu item, and where in the main menu it should be placed.

(b) Suggest an identifier for the button to start and stop logging.

(c) The button itself will not do any of the actual logging: that *has* to be done in the event handler when each new measurement becomes available. All the button can do is to indicate whether writing to the log file should take place or not. An additional data item would be useful to indicate whether logging is taking place. Suggest an identifier for it. (You might like to consider how to avoid having to introduce this additional data item.)

(d) Design the new event handler for the button that will be required. Why is there no need to design an event handler for the new menu item?

(e) Design any additional initialisation steps that will be required.

Exercise 2.4

Describe briefly what changes will be needed to the *OnTimer* event handler to take account of the existence of the variable *Logging*.

Exercise 2.5

Consult the Builder Help system entry for the *TMenuItem* class and decide which property will be useful for indicating that logging is on or off.

[*Solutions on page 38*]

You are now asked to implement the designs just completed. No new components or concepts are required.

Computer Activity 2.2

Open the project `Therm2.bpr` and use `File|Save Project As...` to save it under the new name `Therm3.bpr`. Make sure that the form file `Therm2U.cpp` is the active tab in the Code Editor and use `File|Save As...` to save it as `Therm3U.cpp`.

Edit the main menu to provide the new menu item, as follows. Double-click on the menu *icon* to open the Menu Editor. Highlight the `Exit` item and then press the `Insert` key twice. This will create two blanks above the `Exit` item, one for the new item (Log to File) and one for a separator line (produced by entering a minus '−' sign for the item). Select each blank in turn and enter the items.

Drop a button onto the form and set its *Name* and *Caption* properties.

Create the skeleton *OnClick* event handler by double-clicking on the button. Enter the code for the design created in Exercise 2.3(d). (The drop-down list at the top of the Object Inspector will show what identifier Builder has given to the new menu item. You will need to know this so that you can set its *Checked* property correctly.)

Link the new menu item to the appropriate event handler.

(a) Where should the declaration of *Logging* be placed?

> The caption property is given in step 2 of the initialisation design in the solution to Exercise 2.3(e).

Add the declaration of *Logging*, and modify the *OnTimer* event handler to include an

```
if (Logging) ...
```

statement.

Create the *OnCreate* event handler skeleton and add code to initialise *Logging* correctly.

(b) Run the new version and check that the new button does control logging as required. For now, you can check this by using the Code Editor to view the log file, as you did in Computer Activity 2.1. (A more sophisticated method — a log file viewer — will be discussed in Section 3.)

[*Solution on page 45*]

This latest addition to the program has given the operator better control over what is logged and when. (In some safety-critical computer systems, it may be very undesirable to allow logging to be turned off.)

The next stage is to enable the operator to choose the name of the file to be used for logging. From the design point of view, there are only a few decisions to be made. The logical place to add the file-naming facility is on the File menu. For consistency with other *Windows* programs, two options would normally be offered.

1. File|New... to create a new log file.
2. File|Open... to allow the use of an existing file.

As you will see shortly, you can specify that, for File|New... the file chosen may exist, whereas for File|Open... you can specify that the file *must* exist.

> There is no harm in the user treating File|New... as if it were File|Open....

At present, the name of the file to be used is a string constant "TempLog.dat". This constant needs to be replaced by a string variable. There is one final design decision. What should be done about initialising the file name variable? Before any attempt is made to use the file for logging a measurement, the variable must hold a file name. The decision was made earlier to have logging *disabled* at initialisation, so the event handler for enabling logging *could* check to see if a file name is available and, if not, ask the operator for one. This requires that the file name variable be initialised to the empty string. Another possibility is that the file name variable is set to a default name, such as the one used so far. The course team has opted for the second possibility: initialise to a default name.

> See the solution to Exercise 2.3(e) for 'logging disabled'.

If the identifier *FileName* is used for the string variable holding the name of the current log file, then, since it does not matter whether the file exists or not, a top-level design for the action to be taken when the operator chooses File|New... is as follows.

File|New...

1   get *FileName* from operator

Exercise 2.6

Design the action to be taken when the operator chooses `File|Open`....

[*Solution on page 39*]

Tasks such as those represented by the design in the solution of Exercise 2.6 are standard *Windows* ones. From your work with Builder and other *Windows* programs, you will be used to the dialog boxes that appear in response to `File|Open`... menu items. These are fairly sophisticated *Windows* components which enable the program user to navigate to a desired folder, select an existing file or name a new file to be created. That is, these dialog boxes implement the type of design that is required.

In general, a 'dialog box' is a window which appears and requires that the user interacts with it before the program will continue. The user interaction may simply be to close the dialog box.

To implement the design ideas discussed, the following steps are required.
- The additional items must be added to the `File` menu.
- The *FileName* variable must be declared
- The initialisation of *FileName* must be coded.
- The *OnTimer* event handler code which writes to the log file must be modified to use the file named in the *FileName* variable.
- A dialog box must be added for use by each new menu item event handler.
- Each menu item event handler must be written.

The last two listed steps raise important points. First, the requirements for the dialog boxes are almost, but not quite, the same for `File|New`... and `File|Open`.... In the second case, the file must exist and an error message should appear if it does not. The dialog boxes provided by Builder can have an option set for this purpose, so one solution is to use two dialog boxes, one for `New` and one for `Open`. However, two dialog boxes would use more resources than strictly necessary, so a solution using only one is theoretically better. Second, the code for writing to the log file would not have required any modification if the need for a *FileName* variable had been anticipated earlier. *FileName* could have been introduced right from the start and initialised to the value `"TempLog.dat"`. As a matter of principle, if there is even the remotest possibility of replacing a constant value by a variable at some future time, then an initialised variable should be used right from the start.

Exercise 2.7

(a) Where should *FileName* be declared?

(b) Where will the initialisation of *FileName* be coded?

[*Solution on page 39*]

The revised code for the *OnTimer* event handler of the form *ought* to be something like the following.

```
// display code omitted
....
if (Logging)
{
  LogFile.open(FileName, ios::app);
  LogFile << Thermometer->Value << endl;
  LogFile.close();
}
```

Unfortunately, the `fstream` library cannot deal with names given as
*AnsiString*s, they must be converted using a method (of *AnsiString*) called
c_str. The code has to be as follows.

The Help system entry for this method describes the method as converting the *AnsiString* to a (null-terminated) character array. This is the original way in which C represented strings.

```
// display code omitted
....
if (Logging)
{
  LogFile.open(FileName.c_str(), ios::app);
  LogFile << Thermometer->Value << endl;
  LogFile.close();
}
```

The top-level designs for the `File|New...` and `File|Open...` items refine as follows. The two designs can be essentially the same, only some options of the dialog box will need adjusting for the different handlers.

File|New...

1.1   display dialog box with appropriate options to allow new file name
1.2   **if** user closes the dialog box with the `Open` button **then**
1.3   set *FileName* to string provided by user in dialog box
1.4   **ifend**

If the user chooses the `Cancel` button, nothing needs to be done.

File|Open...

1   **loop**
2.1   display dialog box with appropriate options to require user to choose name of existing file
2.2   **if** user closes the dialog box with the `Open` button **then**
2.3   set *FileName* to string provided by user in dialog box
2.4   **ifend**
3   **loopend when** *FileName* is an existing file

As you will see, the loop coding is not done explicitly.

Coding these will depend on the dialog box class having methods which display the box and enable the programmer to know whether the user pressed the `Cancel` or the `Open` button. Builder provides the *TOpenDialog* class for the current type of task.

The next activity deals with the coding of the log file designs. It is fairly long because there are a number of things to be dealt with; they will be done in the order listed on page 18.

19

Computer Activity 2.3

Open the project `Therm3.bpr` and use `File|Save Project As...` to save it under the new name `Therm4.bpr`. Make sure that the form file `Therm3U.cpp` is the active tab in the Code Editor and use `File|Save As...` to save it as `Therm4U.cpp`.

Double-click on the main menu icon on the form (not the menu itself) to start the Menu Editor. Highlight the `Log to File` item and press the Insert key three times, to give three new, blank items. Selecting each blank item in turn, place the `New...` and `Open...` menu items on the `File` menu, followed by a separator line, above the `Log to File` item. Close the Menu Editor.

A minus sign '−' will produce a separator line.

Name the menu items "New" and "Open".

(a) Check that the project compiles correctly but that the new menu items do nothing.

Add the declaration of *FileName* to the header file `Therm4U.h`, and modify the initialisation code in the way discussed above. Also make the changes discussed to the *OnTimer* event handler code.

(b) Run the new version of the project, and check that logging to `TempLog.dat` is still working.

From the `Dialogs` tab of the Builder component palette, select an *OpenDialog* component and drop it onto the program's form (it will appear as a square icon). Set its *Name* property to *FileDlg*. (Note, from the Object Inspector, that *FileDlg* is an instance of the class *TOpenDialog*.)

The icon is of a file folder.

(c) The dialog box has no *Caption* property. Which property has replaced it?

(d) Which property represents the file name chosen by the operator? Will this cause a problem, given the choice of identifier just declared above?

(e) Consult the Builder Help system for the methods available in the *TOpenDialog* class. Which of the non-derived ones will enable you to implement the **if** step in the event handler design?

(f) Create the event handler skeletons for the `File|New...` and `File|Open...` menu items. Code the design for the event handlers (the same code in each case).

Selecting the menu items whilst viewing the form is probably the easiest way.

(g) Run the revised version. Check that choosing each new menu item produces the dialog box. Choose `Cancel`. Start and stop measurements and check that they have been logged to `TempLog.dat`. Leave the program running, with measurements stopped.

Start logging.

(h) Choose `File|New...` and type a new name into the file name box. Close the dialog box with the `Open` button. Check that measurements are now logged to your new file, and then close that file. Leave the program running, with measurements stopped.

(i) Choose `File|Open...` and, this time, select `TempLog.dat` by double-clicking. (This should also close the dialog box.) Check that measurements are now logged to `TempLog.dat`. Close the program, but leave the project open.

[*Solution on page 45*]

The current state of the monitoring program has two details that really need attention. First, the default title 'Open' (of the dialog box) is not very descriptive and should be set appropriately for the two different uses of the dialog box. Second, nothing has been done to enforce the existence of the file chosen when using `File|Open...`. Fixing both of these has to be done by code, not by setting properties, as different things are required in the two handlers which use the dialog box.

Computer Activity 2.4

In each of the event handlers which use the dialog box, add a line of code to set the *Title* property appropriately. Compile and test your revised version.

Computer Activity 2.5

This activity changes one of the *Options* properties of the dialog box so that the dialog box for `File|Open...` requires that the file exists.

In the event handler for `File|Open...` add the following line of code before the existing code.

```
FileDlg->Options << ofFileMustExist;
```

In the event handler for `File|New...` add the following line of code before the existing code.

```
FileDlg->Options >> ofFileMustExist;
```

These may remind you of file insertion and extraction operators. The *Options* property of a file dialog box has many values, each of which can be set to be 'active' or not. The first line of code you added ensures that the `ofFileMustExist` option is in the set of active options. The second line of code removed the `ofFileMustExist` option from the active set. These are the code equivalents of setting the corresponding entry in the Object Inspector to **true** or **false**, respectively.

Run the revised project and check that attempting to type in the name of a non-existent file produces an error message when using `File|Open...`.

Computer Activity 2.6

This activity adds a feature normally provided by *Windows* file dialog boxes — the provision of a list of file types.

Click on the dialog box icon in the form. In the left-hand column of **Properties** in the Object Inspector, click on the *Filter* property. In the right-hand column, click on the ellipsis (three dots). This will open a Filter Editor window. In the top left-hand cell, enter the following.

```
Data files (*.dat)
```

In the top right-hand cell (move there with the Tab key), enter `*.dat`. In the second row cells, place `All files (*.*)` and `*.*`. Close the Filter Editor with the `OK` button.

Compile the revised version of the project, and check that you can now select the file types that you wish to display in the file list by using the `Files of type:` drop-down list.

[Solutions on page 46]

> This feature is available in dialog boxes for saving files as well as for opening them.
>
> The left-hand column in the Filter Editor is for descriptions; the right-hand column is used by the dialog box code to select files to be displayed. The solution to this activity contains a brief description of how the two columns are usually completed.

This concludes the addition of data logging to the basic monitoring program. The current solution for the Monitoring problem is perfectly satisfactory as a prototype system. It could be used to consult operators on the form of display that they find most helpful, and to experiment with ways of logging data to files, and so on.

One addition to the prototype system would be useful, as you may have found out already. A way of viewing the log file from *within* the program (rather than using Builder's Code Editor) would be very useful at the testing stage. Adding a log file viewer will be discussed in the next section.

3 A log file viewer

When testing the logging process in the previous section, it would have been very useful to have been able to view the current contents of the log file from within the program. The requirement is easy enough to state: provide a display showing the current contents of the log file.

In fact, implementing the new requirement as just stated is almost as easy as stating it. The log file is a text file and, as you know, Builder provides the *TMemo* and *TRichEdit* classes for displaying text. However, before rushing to the Code Editor, the problem specification and design deserves a little more thought. Some questions need to be answered.

- Should the display be part of the program's main window, or be in a separate window?
- The display and the *OnTimer* event handler both require access to the same file. Should logging be temporarily suspended (if it is active) before displaying the file?
- If a separate window is used, should it be permanently open or opened only on request?
- If a separate window is used, should it be a child window (as used in the multi-window warehouse interface) or a normal window? Might it be a dialog box that has to be closed before returning to the main program?

As usual, there are no 'correct' answers to such questions. The course team feels that, on balance, information required only occasionally should be displayed in a separate window. To make maximum use of existing code, it is probably better not to change to a main form plus child form design. It is suggested that you use a dialog box for the viewer. The course team suggests that the window is opened only on request, and that you use a dialog box type window.

As far as dual access to the log file is concerned, it is probably safe not to disable logging whilst viewing the data. The reason is that only the *OnTimer* event handler requires *write* access to the file. Problems usually occur when several different pieces of code are all trying to write to the same file.

This discussion suggests the following specification for the new facility.

Problem Specification   Log File Viewer

A new `File` menu item `View Log File` is to be provided. Selection of this menu item should cause a window to appear which displays the contents of the log file at the time that the window opens. The new window should provide, at least, a button to close the window. (Any window comes with a cross icon for closing it. The use of a button for this purpose is common, and is potentially more versatile.)   □

Exercise 3.1

(a) Give a top-level design for the `File|View Log File` menu item's event handler.

(b) Sketch the visual appearance of the log file viewer window.

[*Solution on page 40*]

The course team solution to Exercise 3.1 will be used as the basis for what follows.

You have already explored (in *Unit 2*) the components that Builder makes available for text display. For this problem, you are asked to use the following data table.

Type	Identifier	Description
TForm	*ViewForm*	Provides the window for the display
TPanel	*ButtonPanel*	For grouping any buttons used to indicate that viewing is finished with
TButton	*OKButton*	Closes window (when viewing finished with)
TMemo	*Viewer*	Displays text of log file

Exercise 3.2

What property of *ViewForm* will you use to control when the window is displayed?

Exercise 3.3

The textual content of *Viewer* is held in its *Lines* property, which is an object of type *TStrings*. By consulting the Help system entry for *TStrings*, locate a method that will help get the contents of the log file into *Lines*.

Exercise 3.4

Give a detailed design (based on the above discussion and the top-level design in the solution to Exercise 3.1) for the event handler which will display the log file contents.

Exercise 3.5

What should the effect be when the user presses the *OKButton* in the *ViewForm* window? How might this effect be achieved?

[*Solutions on page 40*]

The coding of the new features is straightforward. A new unit will have to be added to the project for the new form and its code.

Computer Activity 3.1

Open the project `Therm4.bpr` and save a new version using `Therm5.bpr` for the project and `Therm5U.cpp` for the form file.

Use `File|New Form` to create a new form for the project. Save this form file as `Therm5U2.cpp`. Drop a panel, a button and a memo onto the new form, and set the *Name* properties to reflect the data table given above.

(a) Are there any other properties that you might wish to set?

Set the properties discussed in the solution to part (a).

Switch to the Code Editor (F12) and click on the tab for `Therm5U.cpp`. Switch to the main form and add `File|View Log File` to the menu, via the Menu Editor.

Alternatively, you can use View|Units to open Therm5U.cpp.

(b) Check that the project will run with the latest changes. Select the new form from the menu. Explain what you observe.

Create an event handler skeleton for selection of the new menu item. Add code implementing the design for the event handler, preceded by the following code which tests for existence of a named file.

```
if (FileExists(FileName))
```

The function FileExists is contained in a library supplied with Builder, and is automatically available.

(c) Run the revised project. If compilation fails, correct the problem by adding an appropriate `#include` statement.

Switch back to *ViewForm* and double-click on the button to create its event handler skeleton.

(d) Add code to make the button close the *ViewForm* window.

(e) Run the revised project and test the log file viewer. Can you suggest an addition that would make the viewer more useful?

(f) Set the *Viewer* memo's *ScrollBars* property to a more useful value and retest the project.

[*Solution on page 47*]

The remaining task is to make the display window (*ViewForm*) into a dialog box. The present solution allows you to return to the main window without closing the display window.

Computer Activity 3.2

Open `Therm5.bpr`, if necessary, and change the *BorderStyle* property of *ViewForm* to `bsDialog`.

(a) Run the revised project and check that the display window is no longer resizeable (typical of dialog boxes).

(b) In the `File|View Log File` menu item event handler, *change* the line of code which makes the display window visible to the following.

```
ViewForm->ShowModal();
```

Run the revised version of the project, select `View Log File` and check that you cannot now make the main window active by clicking on it. Check that the main window does become active once the display window has been closed.

[*Solution on page 47*]

The *ShowModal* method is provided for exactly the purpose for which it has just been used: to display a window which must be closed before the user can continue with normal use of the program. Using *ShowModal* enables the programmer to exert the same sort of control over the user that was possible when writing console applications. Excessive use should be avoided, since *Windows* program users prefer to feel in charge of the program.

As you may suspect, the *Execute* method of file open dialog boxes, which you used in Section 2, uses *ShowModal* to insist on some sort of action by the user.

This section has added a useful facility to the prototype monitoring system. In the next section, a different form of log file viewer is considered, leading to some further ideas about displaying data graphically.

4 Data display

The log file viewer provides useful, detailed information about the measurements from the instrument. For some purposes, a graph showing trends in the data, rather than the values of measurements can be valuable. Thus, an alternative, graphical, log file viewer could be a further addition to the monitoring program. In this section, you are asked to tackle a slightly more general version of this task, by designing and coding a separate program which reads and displays data in a file.

The intention is that you should concentrate on the display part of the task, so the reading of the data is delegated to a *DataEngineType1* class which is provided by the course team. The declaration of the class is as follows.

```
class   DataEngineType1
{
// data fields
private:
   int Maximum; // Maximum value of data read
   int Minimum; // Minimum value of data read
   int NumberOfItems; // Number of data items read
   int Data[50]; // Array to store data
   int CurrentItem;
   // Index to array data of next item to be returned by the method NextItem.

// methods
public:
   int Max(void);
   // Returns the maximum value of the data stored

   int Min(void);
   // Returns the minimum value of the data stored

   int NextItem(void);
   // Returns next data item (first use gives first data item)
   // Works as circular list, cycling round the available data
```

This class name has the ending `Type1` to distinguish it from `DataEngineType2` which occurs in *Unit 4*. This latter class is more versatile because the restriction to integers is removed.

```
    bool Init(AnsiString FileName);
    // Reads data from file
    // Returns true if all went well; returns false
    // if file does not exist (Size will return 0 in this case),
    // or if too many data items (Size will return 50)

    int Size(void);
    // Returns number of data items
};
```

The individual data items are accessible only via methods of the class, as usual.

The problem which you are asked to solve is the following.

Problem Specification   Simple graph

A data file contains a maximum of 50 integer values. A program is required to plot these values, in the order of occurrence in the data file, as points joined by straight lines. No axes or scales are to be provided, the purpose is just to get an overall view of trends in the data. (Adding axes and scales is not difficult, but the details will distract from the main ideas involved.)

The program should use an object of the *DataEngineType1* class to read the data file (called **IntData.dat**) and should display the data read in the client area of the program window in response to the user choosing a suitable menu item.   □

From the design point of view, the task is to produce a display of the following form. (Note that underlines have been added to the menu item names.)

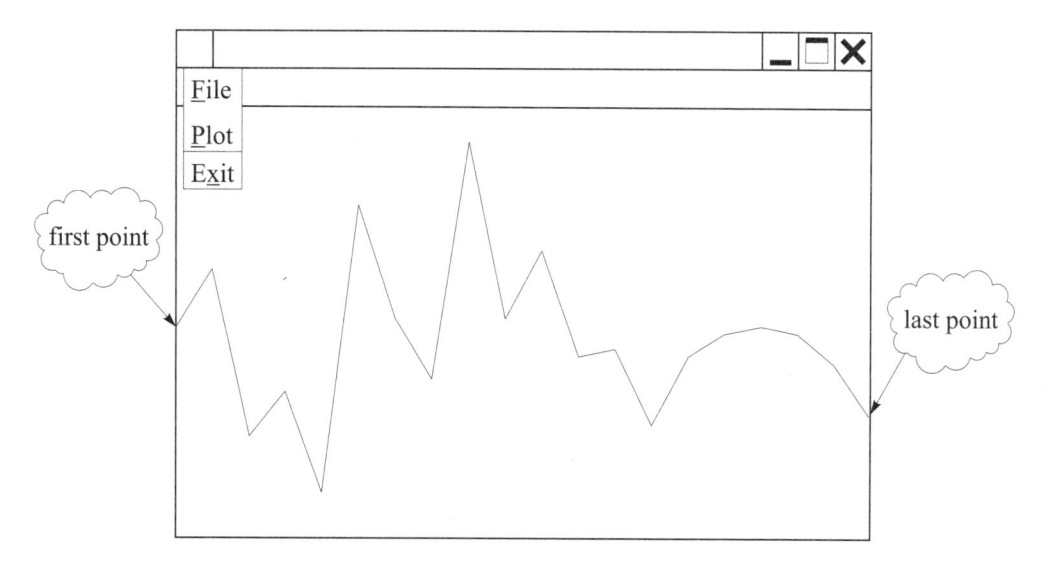

In this figure, which shows 20 data values, no dots have been drawn for individual points. Apart from the first and last points, the position of any point is indicated by the meeting of two line segments. Such a display is sufficient to show any trends in the data.

This specification does not give a number of details. For example, how much of the available area should the graph occupy? What should happen if the user moves or resizes the window? To begin with, a simple approach will be taken and possible further development indicated at the end of the section.

There is a graph component available in the Builder toolkit. It is a very flexible component and its use for this problem would involve a number of properties and methods whose purpose is not immediately obvious. The simplified approach suggested here will introduce you to some very useful properties and methods associated with forms. These properties and methods will be further exploited in Block IV.

Chartfx on the `ActiveX` tab.

To meet the problem specification, the `File|Plot` menu item event handler has to do the following things: cause the data engine to read the data file, obtain the data from the engine and display it in the required way. (This all-in-one approach will be commented on later.) A first attempt at a top-level design could be as follows.

File|Plot

1   initialise data engine from `IntData.dat`
2   **loop** for all data items
3   obtain and display data item (using line segments)
4   **loopend**

Exercise 4.1

(a) Why is this first attempt not quite complete?

(b) Write a revised top-level design which takes account of the solution to part (a).

[*Solution on page 41*]

The subsequent work will be based on choosing to display the data read, even if there was more in the file than the data engine can cope with. In such a case, the class declaration says that the *Init* method will return **false**, but the *Size* method will give a value of 50.

By inspecting the revised top-level design and the declaration of the data engine class, it is possible to draw up a first attempt at a data table. The data engine can provide the number of data items available, so a **for** loop, controlled by an integer variable would be a good way of implementing the loop of the design.

Type	Identifier	Description
DataEngineType1	*DataEngine*	Data engine object
Boolean	*Initialised*	Records whether initialisation was successful enough for data to be displayed
Integer	*Count*	**for** loop counter

Exercise 4.2

Using the data table above, refine steps 1 to 3 of the design in the solution to Exercise 4.1. The variable *Initialised* will be used in the refinement of steps 1 and 2.

[*Solution on page 41*]

The remaining task is the heart of the design: obtaining and displaying each data item in turn. Obtaining the data items is straightforward: the *NextItem* method has been provided for exactly this purpose, calling it *Size* times will provide all the data items. Displaying the data items requires a short digression.

How would the task be done using pen and graph paper? By looking at the quantity of data, you could decide how to space out the points horizontally. For example, if you have 50 data items and graph paper with 200 horizontal divisions, you could allocate 4 divisions to be placed between consecutive items. If the maximum data item was 98 (and you wanted the scale to display 0), and 100 vertical divisions were available, the vertical scale could be one to one. If the first three data items were 50, 27 and 72, they would appear as follows on the specified graph paper.

The data file `IntData` has 50 items, and its maximum data item is 98.

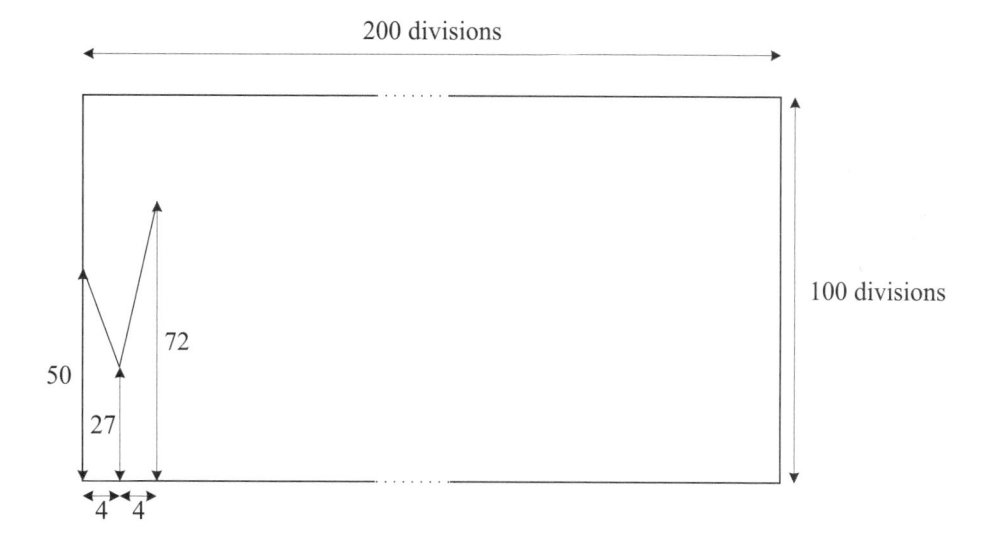

Having decided *where* the points should be, how would the graph be drawn? You would move the pen (without drawing as you go) to the first data point and then draw a line from each data point to the next.

The *TForm* class, from which all forms that you use are descended, provides the *Windows* equivalent of paper and pen. The paper is represented by the form's *Canvas* property which is of the *TCanvas* class. The pen is represented by the *Pen* property of the *TCanvas* class. You will explore the properties of the *TCanvas* class in more detail in Block IV; here, only elementary ideas will be needed.

Borland have chosen to use names based on artists' terms: canvases, pens and brushes.

The *Canvas* (paper) covers the form minus its title bar and menu (if any). This area is called the **client area** of the form. The dimensions of this drawing space are available as the *ClientWidth* and *ClientHeight* properties of the form. Various methods of *TCanvas* allow you to draw on the form; the ones required here are the *MoveTo* and *LineTo* methods.

The individual positions on the canvas are referred to as **pixel** positions. They form a two-dimensional array with indexes running from 0 to *ClientWidth* − 1 horizontally and 0 to *ClientHeight* − 1 vertically. It is these indexes which are the parameters supplied to the *MoveTo* and *LineTo* methods.

'Pixel' is short for 'picture element'; it is the smallest unit (a dot) on the screen. For example, there are *ClientHeight* pixels (i.e. pixel positions) down the screen. The pixel is often used as if it were a unit of distance on the screen.

Computer Activity 4.1

Start Builder, if necessary, and open a new application. Save it in the `Block III` folder as `DrawExp.bpr`.

(a) Look up the description of the methods *MoveTo* and *LineTo* of the class *TCanvas* in the Help system.

Drop a button onto the form, and place it at the top right corner of the form. Change its name to *DrawButton* and its caption to *Draw*. Create the *OnClick* event handler skeleton for this button and place the following code in it.

```
Canvas->MoveTo(0,0);
Canvas->LineTo(100,100);
Canvas->MoveTo((ClientWidth - 1)/2, (ClientHeight - 1)/2);
Canvas->LineTo(ClientWidth - 1, ClientHeight - 1);
```

Since, for example, 17/4 in integer division results in 4, some slight inaccuracy in what is intended may result when using integer division in the *MoveTo* and *LineTo* methods.

Run the project and observe what appears on the canvas when you click the button.

Experiment with changing the numbers in the first two statements. Carry out sufficient experiments so that you can answer the following questions.

(b) Describe the location of the point on the canvas represented by the two numbers 0 and 0.

(c) Write down a statement which would move (without drawing) to the point half-way down the left-hand edge of the canvas.

(d) Write down the statements which would move to the centre of the top edge of the canvas, and then draw a four-sided figure joining the centres of the edges, as shown below.

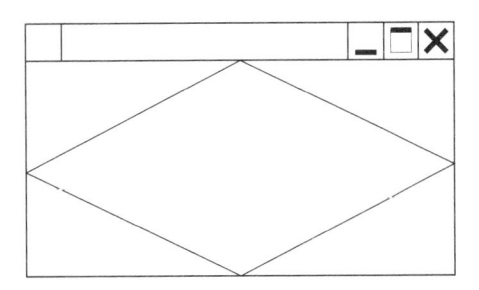

(e) Test your answer to part (d) by changing the button event handler code and running the project.

[*Solution on page 48*]

This digression into the *Canvas* property of forms shows that methods are available to do the drawing of simple line graphs. Knowing this, it is possible to develop the design for a solution to graphing the data stored in a *DataEngineType1* object.

The first data item has to be treated slightly differently from the rest because it must just position the drawing pen, without drawing a line. Subsequent data items will cause a line to be drawn. In view of the special treatment needed for the first data item, the design arrived at in the solution to Exercise 4.2 would be better modified as follows.

1.1 $Initialised \leftarrow DataEngine.Init(\text{``IntData.dat''})$
      or $(DataEngine.Size > 0)$
2.1   **if** $Initialised$ **then**
3.1   obtain first data item and move to corresponding point
3.2   **loop for** $Count \leftarrow 2$ **to** $DataEngine.Size$
4.1   obtain next item and draw line to corresponding point from previous position
5   **loopend**
6   **ifend**

The next stage is to decide exactly which pixel positions on the canvas will correspond to the data items. Here, the canvas will be sized so that it fits the data, rather than adjusting the points to fit the canvas. How to achieve a better solution will be indicated at the end.

The decision will be made to place the first point at the left-hand edge and to move 4 pixels horizontally for each successive data point. That requires a total width of $49 \times 4 = 196$ pixels. The first point will have a horizontal pixel index of 0, the second of 1×4, the third of 2×4, and so on. The loop counter $Count$ determines which data point is being plotted, so the horizontal index at any stage will be

There are 50 points, so 49 horizontal shifts of 4 pixels are required.

$(Count - 1) \times 4.$

The vertical position of each point will be determined by the value of the data item, a value of 1 will be plotted 1 pixel up from the bottom edge, and so on. Since the maximum of the supplied data is 98, a total height of 100 pixels will be sufficient. For a canvas 100 pixels high, the vertical index runs from 0 to 99, increasing downwards. Unfortunately, the data points need to be plotted so that increasing values are plotted upwards! A value of 1 is supposed to be plotted 1 pixel up from the bottom, at a vertical index of

$98 = 99 - 1.$

A value of 2 has to be plotted at $97 = 99 - 2$, and so on.

Exercise 4.3

What vertical index corresponds to a value $Next$, say, returned by the method $NextItem$?

$Next$ is just a temporary device.

Exercise 4.4

Use the solution to Exercise 4.3 to refine steps 3.1 and 4.1 of the design. (Assume that an object called $Canvas$ is available for drawing on. $LineTo$ and $MoveTo$ are methods of this canvas.)

[*Solutions on page 42*]

The design for a solution to the plotting problem is now at the following stage.

1.1   *Initialised* ← *DataEngine.Init*("IntData.dat")
           or (*DataEngine.Size* > 0)
2.1   **if** *Initialised* **then**
3.1.1   *Canvas*→*MoveTo*(0, 99 − *DataEngine.NextItem*)
3.1.2   **loop for** *Count* ← 2 **to** *DataEngine.Size*
4.1.1   *Canvas*→*LineTo*((*Count* − 1) × 4, 99 − *DataEngine.NextItem*)
5   **loopend**
6   **ifend**

Exercise 4.5

Write down the C++ code for the final version of the design, as listed above.

Exercise 4.6

(a) Where should *Initialised*, *Count* and *DataEngine* be declared?

(b) Write down their C++ declarations.

[*Solutions on page 42*]

Apart from the code discussed so far, there is some initialisation to do. The course team solution forces the client area of the form to be set 200 pixels wide and 100 pixels high. This can be done using the *ClientWidth* and *ClientHeight* properties of the form at design time.

Computer Activity 4.2

Start Builder, if necessary, and open a new application. Save the project as `GrData.bpr`, in the `Block III` folder.

Add the unit `DataEng1.cpp` to the project, and add the line

`#include "DataEng1.h"`

to the file `GrDataU.h`.

Drop a main menu on the form and edit it to produce the required `File` menu with `Plot` and `Exit` items on it.

Set properties of the form as follows.

Property	Value	Comment
Caption	"Data plotting"	Sets title for form
ClientWidth	200	Discussed above
ClientHeight	150	Discussed above
Position	*poScreenCenter*	Ensures form appears in standard position

Create event handler skeletons for the two menu items. Place the usual `Close();` statement in the one for `Exit`. In the other event handler, place the code which appeared in the solution to Exercise 4.5 and the variable declarations from the solution to Exercise 4.6.

(a) Run the program and test the `Plot` event handler code. Do you have any comments about the program window?

(b) Implement the changes suggested in the solution to part (a). Test the revised project.

What happens if you resize the program window and then choose `File|Plot` again?

[*Solution on page 49*]

The previous activity is as far as you will be taking the plotting problem in code. The solution developed here was sufficient to illustrate the use of some methods of the *TCanvas* class. A proper solution should plot the data to fit the window size available, rather than the other way round, as here. The plot should also be redrawn correctly if the user moves or resizes the program window. As you may have found, the current solution does not do this. Correct redrawing requires the drawing code to be placed in a quite different event handler, as you will discover in Block IV.

In Block IV the *OnPaint* event handler will be used.

In fact, there are things which can be done to improve the program a little. The figure 99, which keeps appearing, is really *ClientHeight* − 1. Replacing all occurrences of 99 by this expression would ensure that the bottom of the program window is treated as the baseline for plotting.

The figure of 4 (later 8) horizontal pixels per point plotted is really the width of the canvas divided by one less than the number of data points, that is

ClientHeight/(*DataEngine.Size* − 1).

Using this expression instead of a fixed number would enable the program to plot data files with different numbers of items.

Organising the data to fit the window vertically is rather more complicated. It involves using the (so far unused) *Max* and *Min* methods of the *DataEngineType1* class.

There is another, perhaps more fundamental, objection to this solution. The data engine object is re-initialised every time the `File|Plot` menu item is selected, even though only one data file is available. In a more complete program, the user would be able to choose the data file, via a `File|Open` menu item. It is in the event handler for this menu item that the data engine should be initialised.

If you have time, and wish to see how to achieve a more flexible solution to the original problem, you can open and run the project `CTPlotter.bpr` in the Block III folder. You should note that the suggestions above require changes which have not been discussed, so do not spend too long inspecting the code.

Objectives

After studying this unit, you should be able to:
- follow instructions to install a supplied component on Builder's Component Palette;
- explain the purpose of a prototype system, and create a simple one from a given specification;
- explain what is meant by 'appending data to a file' in the context of data logging, and open a data file for appending;
- place appropriate code in the event handlers of Builder's events *OnCreate*, *OnDestroy* and *On Timer*;
- add menu items to an existing menu by means of the Menu Editor;
- with guidance, create a viewing window (as a dialog box), with scroll bars where appropriate, for a data file used in a program;
- with guidance, create a graphic display for data in a file (*not* employing Builder's graph component), sized to fit the range of the data;
- in general, demonstrate a growing confidence in using Builder's VCL in creating *Windows* applications;
- use and understand the use of the following terms: data logging, prototype system, appending data to a file, client area, pixel.

Solutions to the Exercises

Section 1

Solution 1.1

The discussion preceding the exercise suggests a menu to provide the `Exit` option and another menu to provide the `Start` and `Stop` options for measurements. The latter menu could be called `Measurement`. The convention in *Windows* is that an `Exit` item always appears under the `File` menu item. A `File` item on the main menu is also the place where file operations for recording measurements can be placed later. Buttons to start and stop measurements are also suggested by the discussion.

There are many alternatives to the above suggestions. A single menu item `Measure` could be provided, with a check mark against it when active. (You may well have seen such menu items used in *Windows* programs.) A single button to start and stop measurements could be used, possibly with a caption which changes appropriately when the button is clicked.

The choice of the form of display is much more subjective. Traditional thermometers have a vertical column of liquid which rises and falls to indicate temperature. To imitate that requires a vertical bar display, whose height represents the temperature. A modern digital thermometer could be imitated by a numeric display, but it is harder to spot the direction and amount of any change quickly with numeric displays. There is no particular reason to have a vertical bar display, it could be horizontal. It would also be possible to use some sort of circular display, imitating a dial. Since a choice has to be made, the course team has chosen to use a vertical bar, with a label. You will appreciate that changing this decision is a straightforward task when using Builder, you just change some properties (or choose a different component) and make whatever changes to the code are necessary as a consequence.

The course team version of the program window design is as follows.

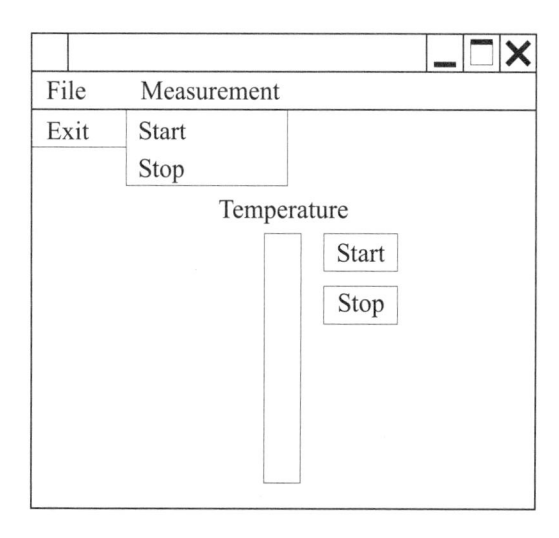

Solution 1.2

The visual and non-visual items are somewhat interdependent. If the measuring instrument is disabled to begin with, then the `Stop` button ought to be disabled too. The `Start` button should be enabled.

The description of *TThermometer* shows that the measuring range has to be set by specifying *Max* and *Min*. A general design is as follows.

1   disable measuring instrument
2   disable `Stop` button
3   enable `Start` button
4   set measuring range to 20–160°C

All of these can be set as properties. The course team follows the principle of using properties for initialisation where it is practicable. Although the course team has not done so, the menu items could also be enabled and disabled to match the buttons. (It seems to be accepted that menu items may be left enabled if choosing them is harmless, even if doing so does nothing.)

Solution 1.3

The first thing that the `Measurement|Start` menu item, or the `Start` button, should do is to begin measurements. The (currently disabled) `Stop` button now needs to be enabled. Since the `Start` button has no useful purpose now, it may be disabled. This gives the following design.

1   enable measuring instrument
2   disable `Start` button
3   enable `Stop` button

Solution 1.4

The `Measurement|Stop` menu item, or the `Stop` button, should stop measurements. The (currently disabled) `Start` button now needs to be enabled. Since the `Stop` button has no useful purpose now, it may be disabled. This gives the following design.

1   disable measuring instrument
2   disable `Stop` button
3   enable `Start` button

Solution 1.5

The display must be updated to show the new measurement.

1   update display with new measurement

Solution 1.6

The `Exit` menu item must close the program.

1   close program

There is another issue to do with closing the program which is discussed in the text following this exercise.

Solution 1.7

The previous designs can now be rewritten using the data table entries. The initialisation has two steps added which set properties of the gauge. (Note that the initialisation design here provides a checklist for setting properties in the Object Inspector, not by writing code.)

> Builder generates code corresponding to setting properties in the Object Inspector.

Initialisation (by setting properties)

1.1 $StopButton {\rightarrow} Enabled \leftarrow$ **false**
2.1 $StartButton {\rightarrow} Enabled \leftarrow$ **true**
3.1 $Thermometer {\rightarrow} Enabled \leftarrow$ **false**
4.1 $Thermometer {\rightarrow} Min \leftarrow 20$
4.2 $Thermometer {\rightarrow} Max \leftarrow 160$
5.1 $TempGauge {\rightarrow} MinValue \leftarrow 20$
5.2 $TempGauge {\rightarrow} MaxValue \leftarrow 160$

Measurement|Start

1.1 $Thermometer {\rightarrow} Enabled \leftarrow$ **true**
2.1 $StartButton {\rightarrow} Enabled \leftarrow$ **false**
3.1 $StopButton {\rightarrow} Enabled \leftarrow$ **true**

Measurement|Stop

1.1 $Thermometer {\rightarrow} Enabled \leftarrow$ **false**
2.1 $StopButton {\rightarrow} Enabled \leftarrow$ **false**
3.1 $StartButton {\rightarrow} Enabled \leftarrow$ **true**

OnTimer event handler

1.1 $TempGauge {\rightarrow} Progress \leftarrow Thermometer {\rightarrow} Value$

The single step in the *OnTimer* event handler causes the current measurement to be assigned to the current value of the display.

File|Exit

1.1 *Close*

The *OnDestroy* event handler has to disable measurements.

OnDestroy event handler

1 $Thermometer {\rightarrow} Enabled \leftarrow$ **false**

Section 2

Solution 2.1

Each measurement has to be written to the file when it becomes available. Displaying the data occurs in the *OnTimer* event handler for the *Thermometer* component. Writing each temperature value to disk should take place just before (or just after) displaying it. (The course team solution will place writing data to file just before displaying it.)

Solution 2.2

```
LogFile.open("TempLog.dat", ios::app);
LogFile << Thermometer->Value << endl;
LogFile.close();
```

This solution uses the *endl* manipulator to place a new line after each data item. The same result can be achieved by inserting `"\n"`. The fact that this alternative does not flush the file is unimportant here as the file is immediately closed, which does flush it.

'Flushing' files is explained in BlockII, *Unit 4*.

Solution 2.3

(a) The suggestion is `Log to File`. Since it is a file operation, it should probably be placed on the `File` menu. There is an arguable case that it is a measurement operation and so should be on that menu. The course team has chosen the first option.

(b) The course team suggests *LogButton*.

(c) A suitable data item is a boolean variable, for which the course team will use the identifier *Logging*.

This additional identifier could be avoided by testing whether or not the `Log to File` menu item was active or not, or equivalently, whether the button was 'on' or 'off'.

(d) The button must set *Logging* **true** or **false** as appropriate, and change its own caption. It should also mark the corresponding menu item as active or not. This is done by placing a check mark on the menu item.

LogButton

1   **if** *Logging* **then**
2   *Logging* ← **false**
3   set button caption to "Start logging"
4   set menu item unchecked
5   **else**
6   *Logging* ← **true**
7   set button caption to "Stop logging"
8   set menu item checked
9   **ifend**

The menu item can be linked to the same event handler, so only one handler is required.

(e) The initial states of *Logging*, the button and the menu item will have to be set. The course team choice is to have 'logging disabled' initially, as described by the following steps, which are the same as in the body of the **if** statement of the *LogButton* event handler.

1   *Logging* ← **false**
2   set button caption to "Start logging"
3   set menu item unchecked

As you will see, step 3 is a default setting in the Object Inspector.

The value of *Logging* will have to be set by code (in the *OnCreate* handler) since it is not a property.

Solution 2.4

The steps which open the file, write to it and then close the file need to be part of an **if** statement using *Logging* to test whether the writing to file should happen. If *Logging* is **false**, the file steps should be skipped.

Solution 2.5

The Builder Help system entry for *TMenuItem* indicates that setting the *Checked* property to **true** places a check mark against a menu item. Thus, code such as

```
MenuItem->Checked = true;
```

will be useful.

Solution 2.6

Here the file must already exist, so a little more thought is needed. A top-level design is as follows.

File|Open...

1 **loop**
2   get *FileName* from operator
3 **loopend when** *FileName* is an existing file

Fortunately, although the design needs a loop, the components made available by Builder provide a way to avoid coding an actual loop.

Solution 2.7

(a) *FileName* is required by more than one event handler, so should be declared (as a string) in the **private** section of the class declaration for the program's form (*TThermForm*). The correct section is **private** because *FileName* is needed only by methods (including event handlers) belonging to this class.

(b) The initialisation of *FileName* (to `TempLog.dat`) may be placed with other coded initialisation, in the *OnCreate* event handler.

Section 3

Solution 3.1

(a) The event handler must display the new window and load the contents of the log file into the window. In theory, these steps could be done in either order, but think for a moment about a dialog-type display window. These are displayed and must be closed before the program can continue executing. If the window is displayed first, the file loading code would not be reached until the window was closed! Thus, to cover both choices of display window type (normal or dialog box), the safest design is as follows.

1. load log file contents into window
2. display window

(b) The course team sketch is as follows.

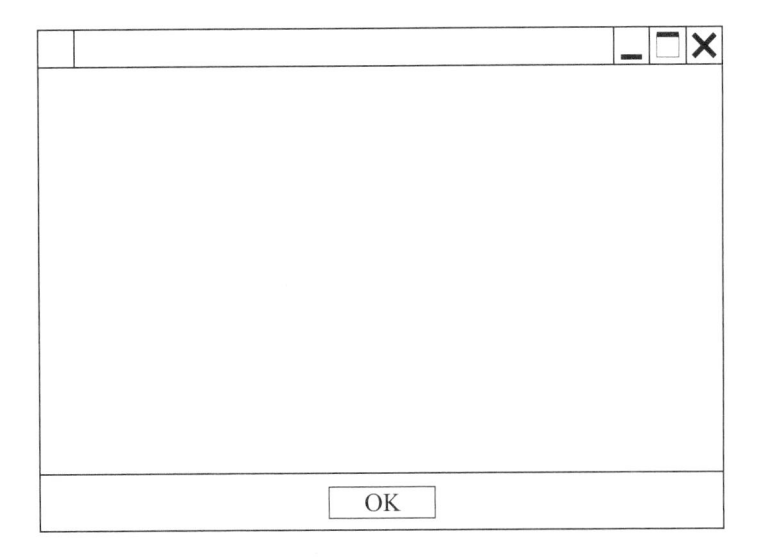

[Sketch of a window with title bar (minimize/maximize/close buttons), a large empty content area, and an OK button at the bottom.]

This sketch envisages the use of an area (implemented as a panel component in Builder) at the bottom with the button on it and a memo area in the middle for the file contents display itself. The panel might seem to be overkill, given that only one button is envisaged. However, there are two reasons to include a panel. First, more buttons might be added later. Second, the window design ideas discussed in the next section would permit the appearance of the various components to be improved more easily if a panel is used to contain the button.

Solution 3.2

The obvious property is *Visible*, which controls whether the form actually appears on the *Windows* desktop.

Solution 3.3

The class *TStrings* has a *LoadFromFile* method. This method is exactly what is required.

Solution 3.4

The following design implements the discussion so far.

1.1   *ViewForm*→*Viewer*→*Lines*→*LoadFromFile*(*FileName*)
2.1   *ViewForm*→*Visible* ← **true**

Because this handler will be in the main form, not in *ViewForm*, the references have to be complete (that is, starting from *ViewForm*). Also, the current name of the log file is in the *AnsiString* variable *FileName*.

Solution 3.5

The *ViewForm* window should disappear. To achieve this effect, either the *Close* method can be used, or the *Visible* property can be set to **false**. The latter approach is consistent with the previous solution, but the *Close* method is the generally adopted approach. (Note that for a form which is not the program's main form, *Close* simply closes the associated window, not the program.)

Section 4

Solution 4.1

(a) The data engine may fail to read the data file correctly, either because the file does not exist or because it contains more than 50 data items. In the first case, there should be no attempt to obtain and display the data. In the second, there is the option to display the 50 items which will have been read. For this problem, you are asked to display any data (up to a maximum of 50 items) which is read.

(b) A revised top-level design is as follows.

    1   initialise data engine from `IntData.dat`
    2   **if** there is data to be displayed **then**
    3   **loop** for all data items
    4   obtain and display data item
    5   **loopend**
    6   **ifend**

Solution 4.2

Refining step 1 will use the *Init* method of the data engine. Deciding whether there is data to display will require the return value from *Init* and a check on the value given by the *Size* method. Even if *Init* returns **false**, there is data to be displayed if *Size* gives a value greater than zero. (You could check for the specific value 50, but that would not be adaptable to future engines capable of handling more than 50 items.) Summing up, there is data to display if *Init* returns **true** or *Size* returns a positive value. Thus, step 1 can be refined as

1.1   *Initialised* ← *DataEngine.Init*("IntData.dat")
              or (*DataEngine.Size* > 0)

The operator **or** *was defined in Unit 2 of Block I.*

With *Initialised* correctly set, step 2 can be refined as follows.

2.1   **if** *Initialised* **then**

The loop has to execute *Size* times. Although it is not the only possibility, the course team have chosen to use the values 1 to *Size*, rather than, say, 0 to $Size - 1$. Thus, step 3 can be refined as follows.

3.1   **loop for** $Count \leftarrow 1$ **to** $DataEngine.Size$

Solution 4.3

The value of the data item has to be subtracted from 99 (the value at the bottom of the canvas), so the vertical index is

$99 - Next.$

Solution 4.4

For step 3.1, a move (without drawing) has to be made to

0 (horizontal index), $99 - Next$ (vertical index)

so the refinement is as follows.

3.1.1 $Canvas \rightarrow MoveTo(0, 99 - DataEngine.NextItem)$

From the earlier discussion, the horizontal position inside the loop is given by

$(Count - 1) \times 4$

and the vertical position by

$99 - Next.$

Using *LineTo* will cause a line to be drawn from the previous position to the new one, so the following refinement of step 4.1 does what is required.

4.1.1 $Canvas \rightarrow LineTo((Count - 1) \times 4, 99 - DataEngine.NextItem)$

Solution 4.5

The design translates into C++, line for line, as follows. (There are more braces than strictly necessary.)

```
Initialised = DataEngine.Init("IntData.dat") || (DataEngine.Size() > 0);
 if (Initialised)
 {
   Canvas->MoveTo(0, 99 - DataEngine.NextItem());
   for (Count = 2; Count <= DataEngine.Size(); Count = Count + 1)
   {
     Canvas->LineTo((Count - 1) * 4, 99 - DataEngine.NextItem());
   }
 }
```

Solution 4.6

(a) With the present solution, only the File|Plot event handler uses the variables *Initialised*, *Count* and *DataEngine*, so that is where they should be declared.

(b)
```
bool Initialised;
int Count;
DataEngineType1 DataEngine;
```

Solutions to the Computer Activities

Section 1

Solution 1.1

(a) The `File|Exit` event handler just needs to use the *Close* method (which belongs to the form) as you have done for several other programs. Clicking on the `File|Exit` menu item (whilst viewing the form) will create the skeleton, to which you should have added the line of code

```
Close();
```

to complete it. After compiling, the program should have run correctly and you should now be able to close the program from the menu item.

(b) The naming of options for the gauge *Kind* property is not totally obvious. (The prefix *gk* is for *gauge kind*.) The value *gkVerticalBar* looks promising for the current project. Setting *Progress* to a temporary value of 90, as suggested, will produce a bar in the display to check this assertion. Setting *ShowText* to false removes the text which indicates a percentage.

(c) The properties that appear for the *TThermometer* component are as described in the specification. By default, measurements are disabled and the *Interval* property has the value 1000, meaning that measurements are made every second.

The compiled version should be visually correct but non-functional, except for the `File|Exit` menu item.

(d) The initialisation design provides a checklist of properties and values that should be set in the Object Inspector.

Solution 1.2

(a) The designs translate into code as follows.

```
void __fastcall TThermForm::StartButtonClick(TObject *Sender)
{
    Thermometer->Enabled = true;
    StartButton->Enabled = false;
    StopButton->Enabled = true;
}
//-----------------------------------------------------------

void __fastcall TThermForm::StopButtonClick(TObject *Sender)
{
    Thermometer->Enabled = false;
    StopButton->Enabled = false;
    StartButton->Enabled = true;
}
```

(b) This step requires you to select the menu items (in turn) in the Object Inspector, choose the **Events** tab and use the drop-down list by *OnClick* to select the corresponding button click event handler.

43

(c) The code has to disable the instrument. The following single line is all that is required.

```
Thermometer->Enabled = false;
```

Solution 1.3

The complete course team version of the project is in `CTTher1.bpr`. If you experienced problems, check your code against the course team project.

Solution 1.4

The course team version illustrating some possible additions is in the project `CTTherx.bpr`.

(a) Setting *BorderStyle* to *bsDialog* prevents the window being resized, but also removes the menu, so that the cross icon has to be used to close the program. (It is a *Windows* convention that dialog boxes do not have menus.) The style of *bsNone* also prevents the window being resized, but it removes the title bar. The choice which achieves what is required, with no ill effects, is *bsSingle*.

(b) Setting the label captions at initialisation (rather than in the Object Inspector) would reduce the amount of recoding necessary if ranges of measurements have to be changed at some later time. However, for now, the initialisation of the label captions is done by setting properties.

(c) The *ForeColor* property determines the colour of the bar representing the measurement.

(d) An **if** statement setting *ForeColor* to `clGreen` for an acceptable measurement and to `clRed` otherwise could be used as a warning device. The course team also tested this with a very narrow range of acceptable values: 80–100 and with *Interval* set to 200.

(e) The course team tried all options, and is of the opinion (and that is all it is, an opinion) that a vertical or horizontal bar is more 'natural' for a temperature display. It is worth noting that experimenting with the different visual forms of the gauge component requires no recoding by you, just changing the value of a property.

(f) `Exit` should be changed to `E&xit` to follow conventions. (Convention dictates the use of E<u>x</u>it, not <u>E</u>xit.) The only check that you should make is that there are no clashes. For example, you cannot have S as the shortcut for both the start and stop buttons since both buttons are active at the same time.

(g) The single-button event handler would have to contain code like the following, which assumes that the single button is named *Button*.

```
if (Button->Caption == "Start")
{
  Thermometer->Enabled = true;
  Button->Caption = "Stop";
}
else
{
  Thermometer->Enabled = false;
  Button->Caption = "Start";
}
```

Section 2

Solution 2.1

(a) With the time interval between measurements at 1000 (milliseconds) the course team managed 9 measurements in the first run of about 10 seconds.

If you wish to consult it, there is a complete course team version of this stage of the project in `CTTher2.bpr`.

(b) After the second run, there were 19 measurements in the course team's file. You are quite likely to get a different number of measurements in the two runs. You could reduce the uncertainty by setting *Interval* to 2000 and timing carefully.

Solution 2.2

The complete course team code is in the project `CTTher3.bpr`.

(a) The value of *Logging* is changed by one event handler and read by a second, so must be accessible to several methods of *TThermForm*. It is not required by anything outside the form, so the **private** section of the class declaration is the appropriate place.

The body of the **if** statement in the *OnTimer* event handler should contain just the three statements involved in logging the measurement to the file. The display instruction should be outside the **if** statement.

(b) The course team ran the program a number of times with measurements enabled for about 10 seconds each time. The following combinations were tried in separate tests.

1. Logging not enabled at all.
2. Logging enabled before measurements started and not disabled at all.
3. Logging started before measurements started, but stopped half-way through.
4. Logging started half-way through the measurement period.

In each case, the expected number of measurements were added to the file. (0, about 10, about 5 and about 5, respectively.)

Solution 2.3

The complete course team project is in `CTTher4.bpr` which you can use for comparison.

(a) The only likely causes of error are the usual ones of misspelled identifiers. In the case of the course team, this usually takes the form of incorrect upper- and lower-case letters.

(b) The Code Editor can be used to check the contents of the log file.

(c) The *Title* property corresponds to *Caption* for other components. The course team cannot find a reason for this change.

(d) The *FileName* property contains the name selected or typed in by the operator. There will be no clash with the *FileName* variable declared in the *TThermForm* class. The dialog box property is

```
FileDlg->FileName
```

when referenced outside the implementation of the *TOpenDialog* class.

(e) According to the Help system, the *Execute* method displays the box and returns **true** if the box was closed by selecting the `Open` button, and **false** if the box was closed by selecting `Cancel` (or by pressing the Esc key). This is exactly what is needed.

(f) For now, both event handlers can contain the same code. (Differences will be introduced later.)

```
if (FileDlg->Execute())
   FileName = FileDlg->FileName;
```

will implement either menu item event handler. (Keep the default names for these menu items.)

> You may care to pause and reflect on how much reusable code is hidden in this brief **if** statement!

(g) Again, you can use the Code Editor to check on the log file contents, but you will have to click on Builder's button on the Taskbar to restore the Code Editor to view. (Minimise Builder again when you have inspected the file contents.)

(h) The course team chose the name `NewLog.dat` for the file.

(i) The file dialog box behaved in the expected way and the new measurements were logged to `TempLog.dat`. (Again, the file contents are checked by using the Code Editor.)

Solution 2.4

The course team chose to set the titles as follows. The code

```
FileDlg->Title = "New log file";
```

was placed in the File|New... handler and

```
FileDlg->Title = "Open log file";
```

in the File|Open... handler. Each of these lines should appear *before* the code (using the *Execute* method) which causes the box to be displayed.

> This code, and that relating to Computer Activities 2.5 and 2.6, is contained in the project `CTTher5.bpr`.

Solution 2.5

The changes suggested mean that the file dialog box for File|Open... will not close on clicking `OK` if the file chosen does not exist; instead, an error message appears.

Solution 2.6

The *Filter* property of file dialog boxes provides a list of file types. The left-hand column in the Filter Editor is for descriptions; the right-hand column is used by the dialog box code to select files to be displayed.

> This property is available in dialogs for saving files as well as for opening them.

The descriptions can be whatever you want, but the convention is to place the filter (e.g. `*.dat`) in parentheses after the description. It is also usual to have the 'All files' option as one of the filter expressions. On the right-hand side, the filter expressions are those that would be used at a DOS box command prompt to obtain a directory listing of the required files. For example, the command

```
dir *.dat
```

at the command prompt would produce a listing of `dat` files in the current directory. (The `*` symbol matches any character or characters; the `?` symbol matches any single character.)

Section 3

Solution 3.1

The complete course team solution is in `CTTher5.bpr`. The course team chose to add the new menu item just above the `Log to File` item.

(a) The course team chose to set the *Position* property of the new form to *poScreenCenter* to ensure that it appeared in a sensible place. (Actually, the course team usually sets this property to this value for all forms used: it makes a better default value than the one Builder supplies.)

The *Caption* property for the panel was set to the empty string, and that for the button to 'OK'.

The other settings that the course team used concern the *Align* property of the components, which you met in *Unit 2*. For the panel, this was set to *alBottom* and for the memo to *alClient*.

(b) The main thing that you will have observed was that the new window did not appear. On closing the program, the Object Inspector shows that the default value of *Visible*, for a form which is not the program's main form, is **false**.

(c) The first time that the course team tried to compile this project, there was an error message indicating that *ViewForm* was unknown. This should have been foreseen, since *ViewForm* is in a different unit from the event handler which is trying to use it. Adding

```
#include "Therm5U2.h"
```

to the top of `Therm5U.cpp` solves the problem. The handler code itself is just the C++ version of the two lines in the design, preceded by the file existence test.

(d) The course team chose to use the *Close* method in the button event handler.

(e) By this stage, the course team's log file contained more lines than would fit in the display window. Scroll bars would enable all the text to be viewed.

(f) Setting the *ScrollBars* property to *ssVertical* remedied the defect. Since the individual lines are short, there is no need for a horizontal scroll bar.

Solution 3.2

The course team version of the project at this stage is in `CTTher6.bpr`.

(a) You may find it a little odd that the type of border given to a window also controls other important aspects of its behaviour (such as not being resizeable). This is another example of a convention laid down by the *Windows* environment.

(b) This change to the event handler does have the desired effect.

Section 4

Solution 4.1

(a) The descriptions of *MoveTo* and *LineTo* use the properties *Pen* and *PenPos*. Make sure you have read their descriptions as well.

Clicking the button should have caused two lines to appear as follows.

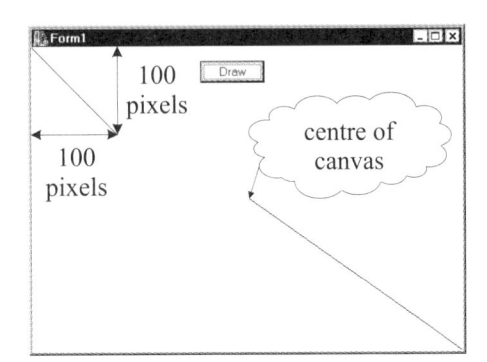

(b) Your experiments should have convinced you of the following.
- The top-left hand corner is described by 0 and 0.
- The first parameter in *MoveTo* or *LineTo* represents the distance across the canvas from the left-hand edge.
- The second parameter in *MoveTo* or *LineTo* represents the distance down the canvas from the top edge.

(c) *MoveTo* is the method which moves the pen without drawing. Points on the left-hand edge are represented by 0, something. The distance down required is $(ClientHeight - 1)/2$, so the statement is

```
Canvas->MoveTo(0, (ClientHeight - 1)/ 2);
```

(The statement must start with `Canvas->` because *MoveTo* is a method of the *TCanvas* class, not of the form.)

(d) Analysing the positions as in the previous part leads to the following code.

```
Canvas->MoveTo((ClientWidth - 1)/2, 0);
Canvas->LineTo(ClientWidth - 1, (ClientHeight - 1)/2);
Canvas->LineTo((ClientWidth - 1)/2, ClientHeight - 1);
Canvas->LineTo(0, (ClientHeight - 1)/2);
Canvas->LineTo((ClientWidth - 1)/2, 0);
```

This code generates the shape in a clockwise sequence from the starting point.

The reason for subtracting one from *ClientWidth* and *ClientHeight* in this code is that the positions in the canvas run from 0 to *ClientWidth* − 1 horizontally, and from 0 to *ClientHeight* − 1 vertically.

(e) Implementing the code in part (d) gave the required results when run.

Solution 4.2

(a) The course team's version of the program (not supplied) produced the following display.

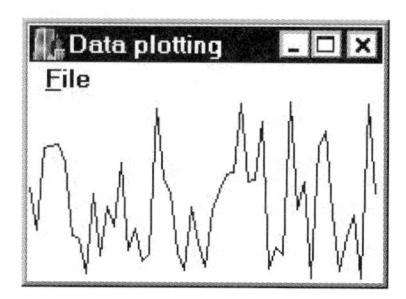

The program window is rather small; it occupies only about one-twelfth of a screen running at the minimum resolution of 640 by 480 pixels.

Doubling the scale of everything results in a slightly better display. To do so, the following changes have to be made.

- *ClientWidth* has to be set to 400.
- *ClientHeight* has to be set to 250.
- The expression

$$(Count - 1) \times 4$$

has to be replaced by

$$(Count - 1) \times 8.$$

- The two occurrences of the expression

$$99 - DataEngine.NextItem$$

have to be replaced by

$$199 - 2 \times (DataEngine.NextItem).$$

(b) The revised code is as follows.

```
Initialised = DataEngine.Init("IntData.dat") || (DataEngine.Size() > 0);
if (Initialised)
{
  Canvas->MoveTo(0, 199 - 2 * DataEngine.NextItem());
  for (Count = 2; Count <= DataEngine.Size(); Count = Count + 1)
  {
    Canvas->LineTo((Count - 1) * 8, 199 - 2 * DataEngine.NextItem());
  }
}
```

The result is a slightly improved display.

This solution does not cope with resizing the program window, as you can confirm by experiment.

Index

adding a component to Builder   10
appending data to a file   14
client area   29
data logging   5, 12

dialog box   18
pixel   29
pixel position   29
prototype system   7